Cover Design: Prince Studio
—adapted by Jason Pollen

Interior Illustrations:
—Prince Studio
—Alan Johnstone
 of Prince Studio
—Jason Pollen
—David Smeaton

LOVE...
an experience of

by
Peter McWilliams

Copyright © 1972, 1974, 1978
by Peter McWilliams. All rights reserved.

Originally published in hard cover by
Doubleday and Company. Reprinted by permission.

ISBN: 0-931580-04-8

Printed in USA

Part One

What is your name?

How will it happen?
How will it happen
when I find some
someone to spend
a goodly portion
of my life with?

It must.
I mean, I've been
pre-pairing
so long . . .

It will happen.
yes.

I will not dwell on
if, only
how, when, where, whom.

this is a
simple
statement
of
loneliness.

a simpler
statement
would be a
scream.

I tried that,
but found it
lacking in
literary
merit.

I reach out to people
and I Touch them
and they respond.

they respond.
they just respond.

Oh God,
how I need someone
to reach out to me.

I don't know
how to lose.

That's part of the problem.

I don't know
how to win either.

That's the other part.

I don't know if
Love conquers All.

I do know it certainly
conquers me with alarming regularity.

Someday we are going to be lovers.
Maybe married.
At the very least, an affair.'

What's your name?

all night long.

laughing.
playing with words
pillows blankets time
each other.

falling in love.
falling asleep.

not making love
until the next
morning and the
birds were singing

you smile.
I forget where I am.
and it takes me longer
each time to remember again.

I don't think
I'll call you
tonight.

I think
I'll take on
another activity
and lose myself
in busy-ness.

you're beginning to mean
too much
to me

and I still don't
know how to
handle that

your
imperfections
only draw me
closer to you.

they remind me
that you're
human.

that with humans
I have a chance.

I know
I love you.

I do not know
which one of us
those words scare
most.

how can I
no
one so wonderful?

how can I
know
one so complex?

yes, do, touch.

yes, please, love.

I will respond
and love & touch
in return.

I know I will want
to touch
when you are gone.

and I will
love you
as you give your
wonders to another.

in that
Impossible Moment
I will write the world
a memorandum,
sharing my sorrow
with fellow fatalities . . .

But tonight
I will enjoy
your
smile
    &
        touch
          &
            words
              &
                love.

   I will not think of
beginnings or endings now.

only of your
        soft
           soft
              soft

I want to
explore the delights
of
one to one
human emotion
with you.

I want to say
whatever words
need be said
to get words
out of the way.

I am impatient.
I am frightened.
I am fascinated.
I am in love with you.

I would like to
know you.
Know you well.

your concepts . . .
where they came from.
where they are taking you.

what it is
that makes
you . . . you.

I already like you.
I'd like to know why.

And since I already
know what lies at
the farthest reach
of your mind,
I will enjoy
the traveling
all the more.

talk
is the language of
friends.

touch
is the language of
loves.

Come.
Become a
linguist
with me.

A FEW FACTS OF LIFE:

Earthquakes level large cities.

Birds lay eggs.

Ice is cold.

An orange is orange.

Dogs bark.

Fire is hot.

Bees fly.

I love you.

Sea water contains salt.

Sharks have sharp teeth.

Flowers grow.

Books are made of paper.

I don't want
to build my
life around
you,

but I want to
include you
in the building
of my life.

Part two:
I find I lost.

I sleep for a while.

wake up feeling
so much love
for you.

write a joyous poem.

dial your number.

no answer.

write a painful poem.

and sleep for a while.

I had all but
forgotten
this feeling.
A survival mechanism
at work, no doubt.

Somehow the months
have constructed a
mental image of
painless love.

Ha!

FEBRUARY ELEVENTH

you're in the kitchen
laughing with your friends.
ha ha.
& I'm in the living room
& the music's too loud
& the only thing to read
is a copy of *Time* I've
already read.

you've made your decision.
you openly plan a party
for next weekend. *our* next
weekend.

I am not overpowered by
all this. a bit surprised
though. And a little saddened:
I wanted someone
to send a Valentine to
this year.

A Valentine thought for you:

"Cupid"
and
"stupid"

rhyme.

I guess this marks
the germination of
our termination.

saying
good night
you
leave,
sentencing
me to a
bad
one.

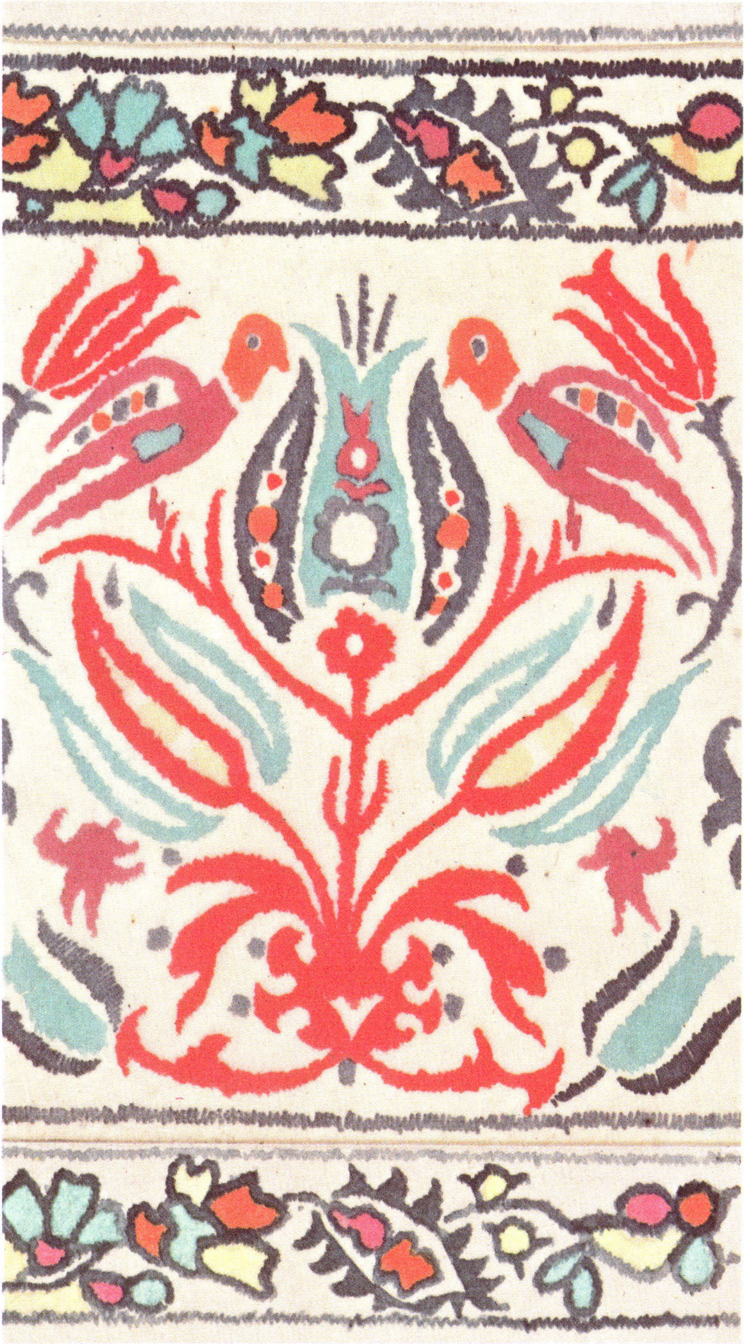

An oyster's
tears turn
to pearls.

A poet's
tears turn
to poems.

Hermann Hesse, from *Steppenwolf:*

*"The man of power is ruined
by power, the man of money
by money, the submissive man
by subservience, the pleasure
seeker by pleasure . . ."*

and me,
by love.

I do all right
alone,
and better
together,
but
I do very poorly
when
semi-
together.

in solitude
I do much,
in love
I do more,
but
in doubt
I only transfer
pain to paper
in gigantic Passion Plays
complete with miracles and martyrs
and crucifixions and resurrections.

come to stay
or
stay away.

this series of passion poems
is becoming a heavy cross to bare.

I'd have a
nervous breakdown
only
I've been through
this too many
times to be
nervous.

I find
I lost.

pain
    is not so heavy
    a burden in
    summer.

walks
    through
    travelogue scenes
    prevent a good
    deal of destruction.

and
    even though no one
    is there to warm me,
    the sun will.

but
    Fall just fell,
    leaving Winter,
    and me
    with no warmth
    within to face
    the cold without.

I might just stick
to the sidewalk
and freeze.

excuse me

I am currently afflicted with the world's number one cripplier

INFATUATION   FIXATION   PARALYSIS

commonly referred to in non-medical circles as

LOVE

any spare COMFORT you have to give would be most appreciated, although my ability to receive may be temporally impaired.

thank you

pain
is
discovering
there
is
nothing
left
to
discover

The fear that I would
come home one day and
find you gone has turned
into the pain of the
reality.

"What will I do if it happens?"
I would ask myself.

What will I do
now that it
has
?

pain
is
the
presence
of
your
absence

                        warm
                        human
                        soft
          next to me in the dark
                        naked
                        body
                        together
                        in a
          not necessarily
                        but
          not necessarily not
                        sexual
                        situation.

                  a human want

                  a want I need

                  since you
                              left
                                    me

                        bleeding.

pain
is
what
burns
when
there's
no
love
to
warm

I ceremoniously disposed
of all the objects connected
with you. I thought they were
contaminated.
                        It did not help.

I'm the one that's contaminated

pain
is
a
beautiful
day
and
no
one
to
share
it
with

It's
dangerous
to leave a
lonely man
alone.

You don't
know what
lies
he'll tell
about you.

Or worse,

what truths.

**pain
is
terminal
loneliness**

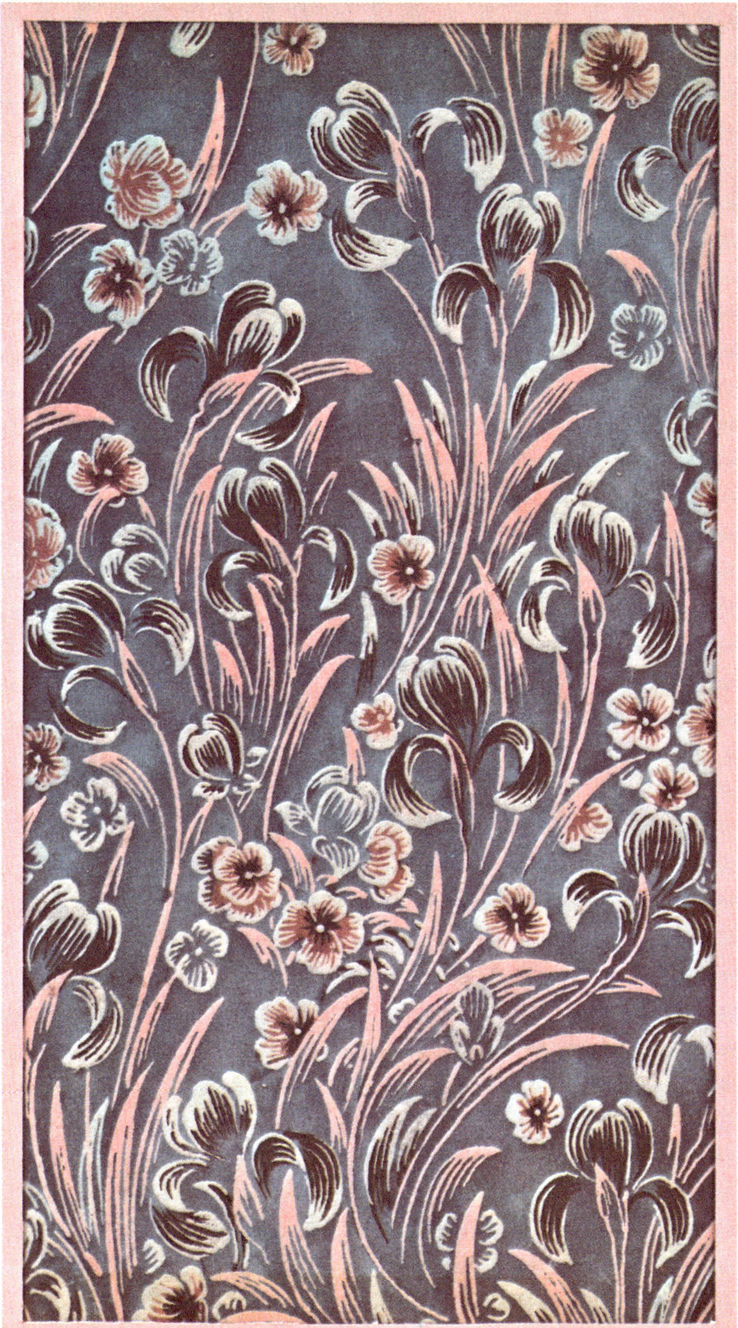

Yesterday was Sunday.
Sundays are always bad.
("Bloody," as they have been
aptly described.)

The full moon is Wednesday.
Full moons are always bad.
(Ask Lon Chaney)

Friday is Good Friday,
and, 30 miles from Rome,
the vibrations of all those mourning
Italians will make it bad.

Sunday is Easter — but it's also
Sunday,
         and Sundays are always bad.

pain
is
any
thought
of
our
joy
together
now
that
we're
apart

Plans:

next month:
> find someone new.

this month:
> get over you.

this week:
> get you back.

today:
> survive.

pain
is
loving
an
objecting
object

She asked me if seeing you was a drain.

Seeing you is not a drain.

It's a sewer.

At first my love for you seemed the
most important force in the universe.

For a while
I loved you well
& it made me well.
("energy flowing through a
system acts to organize
that system.")

The giving of love was so
joyous.
I wanted you to experience
this joy.

So I asked you
to love me,

an impossibility . . .
that turned into a goal,
that turned into a pain,
that drove me insane,
again.

my needs return.
they render me helpless.

and my love for you
seems the most
impotent
force in the universe.

When I
create
something
it doesn't
hurt
as much.

Maybe
that's why
God
created me.

A new morning
of a
new life
without
you.

So?

There will be others.
much finer.
much mine-er.

And until then
there is me.

And because I treated
you
well,
I like me better.

Also, the sun rises.

I hope I heal soon.

I want to enjoy
    Autumn.

You were the best of loves,
you were the worst of loves . . .

and you left behind several
unintended gifts:

through you I re-recognized my
need (uh, desire?) for one significant
other to share my life-space with.

you commanded in me an unwilling
re-evaluation of self, behavior patterns,
relationshipping, & a corresponding
change of attitudes; i.e.: growth.

I'm nicer to people.

I'm more in touch with my feelings,
the things and persons around me, life.

And, of course, a scattering of poems
(the best of poems, the worst of poems)
that never would have happened without
your disruptions.

      Thanks.

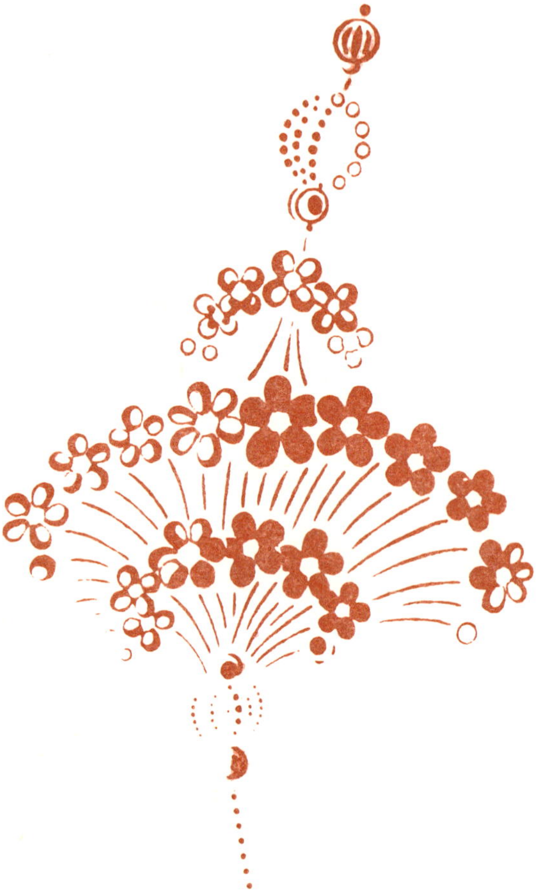

and
through
all the
tears
and the
sadness
and the
pain
comes the
one thought
that can
make
me
smile again:

I Have Loved.

The books in the Peter McWilliams
poetry series are:

VOLUME ONE: Come Love With Me and Be My Life.

VOLUME TWO: For Lovers and No Others.

VOLUME THREE: I Love Therefore I Am.

VOLUME FOUR: The Hard Stuff: Love.

VOLUME FIVE: Love: An Experience Of.

VOLUME SIX: Love Is Yes.

VOLUME SEVEN: Come To My Senses.

and How To Survive The Loss of a Love.
   (with Melba Colgrove, Ph.D.,
   and Harold Bloomfield, M.D.)

Leo Press — Allen Park, Michigan 48101

THE LEO PRESS CATALOG is more a book than a catalog. It features 60 poems, illustrated in full color, as well as information on our books, greeting cards, notecards, postalcards, calendars and whatever else we come up with. It's free. Write for your copy today.